The Famous Dodgers Ballboy

Pierce R. Allen

HERE'S TO THE NEXT GENERATION OF
BASEBALL FANS. PLAY BALL!

CONTENTS

1 THE BASEBALL FAN

In the heart of Pasadena, California, lived a 13-year-old baseball fan named Clay. His world revolved around the crack of the bat, the smell of fresh-cut grass, and the thrill of sliding into home plate. Clay played third base for the Pasadena Pumas, a spirited travel team that took him to different corners of Southern California, facing off against teams like the Malibu Mallards, Glendale Gladiators, and the Long Beach Llamas.

From a young age, Clay was immersed in a family tradition that treated Los Angeles Dodgers baseball as more than just a sport—it was a shared passion. Watching the Dodgers play, hearing the roar of the crowd at Dodger Stadium, and cheering together as a family had created endless memories that defined Clay's love for the team. Inspired by the greatness of players like Clayton Kershaw, who Clay was even named after, Clay found not just heroes on the field but a sense of belonging. The Dodgers were more than a tcam for Clay; thcy were a source of inspiration, joy, and connection.

But Clay wasn't just a fan. On the field he was just as passionate. He took pride in being a tough out at the plate, making pitchers work, and waiting for his pitch. He slapped singles, ripped extra base gappers, and even slugged the occasional home run—though that was rare. However, his true passion was defense. He manned the hot corner at third base with pride, chasing down grounders, snagging one-hoppers, and charging bunts. Clay's enthusiasm for the diamond was at a fever pitch as he anticipated an upcoming Saturday game against the Long Beach Llamas.

2 THE BATBOY PROMOTION

Midweek, Clay and his mother embarked on a shopping adventure to the local sporting goods store. The mission? To find the perfect pair of baseball pants for the upcoming game. In the previous game, Clay had given his all, diving for a ground ball and tearing a hole in his pants. As Clay and his mother made their way from the parking lot to the storefront, an enticing promotion caught their attention – a celebration of all things Los Angeles Dodgers.

A buzz filled the store as Clay eyed the display of Dodgers merchandise. The aisles felt like a playground for Clay, his eyes lighting up as he explored the treasure trove of baseball gear. Amidst the sea of Dodgers blue, a large display promoting a contest captured his interest. Baseball fans aged 12 to 18 had the chance to become the Dodgers Batboy for Sunday's game. To enter the contest, fans must take a quick Dodgers trivia quiz—those that answered all questions correctly would be entered into a drawing to be the lucky winner. Clay's eyes widened with possibility. The dream of being up close and personal with his Los Angeles Dodgers heroes fueled his imagination.

As he tried on new baseball pants, the thrill of the contest lingered in his mind. Clay told his mother that he wanted to enter the contest, and to his excitement she told him they had just enough time to take the trivia quiz.

Eager to dive into the Dodgers promotion, Clay made his way to the front of the sporting goods store where the promotion organizer named Bill was orchestrating the Dodgers trivia quiz. With a confident grin, Clay signed up for the chance to be the Dodgers Batboy. Bill, a Dodgers enthusiast himself, shook Clay's hand for good luck.

"Alright, Clay! You've got 30 seconds to answer five questions. Think fast!" Bill announced with a lively energy.

As the timer started ticking, Clay faced the rapid-fire questions:

"Where were the Dodgers originally located?"

Clay's eyes lit up, and he confidently replied, "Brooklyn, New York!"

"Who courageously broke the color barrier in baseball, by being the first African American to play in the Major Leagues?"

Clay's mind quickly recalled the legendary icon, and

he declared, "Jackie Robinson!"

"In 1963, what player won the Cy Young Award and the Most Valuable Player for the National League?"

Clay's determination shone through as he answered, "Sandy Koufax!"

"When Clayton Kershaw, Corey Seager and the rest of the 2020 Los Angeles Dodgers won the World Series, what team did they beat?"

The recent memory of Dodgers glory fueled Clay's response, "The Tampa Bay Rays!"

As the seconds dwindled away, the tension in the air thickened.

"Last question. We miss him dearly; who is considered to be the greatest baseball broadcaster of all time?"

Clay's heart raced as he named the beloved radio legend just in time, "Vin Scully!"

As the buzzer sounded, Bill exclaimed, "Well done, Clay! You nailed it! You've qualified for the drawing to be the Dodgers Batboy!"

Unable to contain his joy, he turned to Bill, the spirited organizer. "Thanks, Bill! You know, I play for the Pasadena Pumas, and we've got a big game this Saturday. As a fellow baseball fan, you should come watch the game!"

Bill, genuinely thrilled by the teen's enthusiasm, gladly accepted the invitation. "You know what, that sounds like fun. I'll bring my 8-year-old son, he'd love to see how older travel teams play."

3 THE ANNOUNCEMENT

The next few days felt like an eternity for Clay as he anxiously awaited the results of the drawing. Bill, the promotion organizer, had informed Clay and his mom that the winner would be announced during Friday night's Dodgers game. Clay's nerves were on edge, and the ticking clock seemed to echo in his mind.

The rest of the week crawled by, each passing moment adding to the suspense. Friday finally arrived, and the excitement in the air was palpable. Clay piled in the car with his family to go to Dodger Stadium, all eagerly anticipating the big moment. The Dodgers were set to face their archrivals, the San Francisco Giants, in what promised to be a thrilling matchup.

The game unfolded with gripping intensity. In the third inning, the Dodgers electrified their fans as their clean-up hitting catcher smashed a home run, propelling them to a 3-run lead. However, the Giants retaliated in the fourth inning, stringing together some pesky hits to knot the score at 3-3.

Undeterred, the Dodgers veteran pitcher regained control, holding the Giants at bay through the bottom of the seventh inning. Not another hit or run slipped through his expert fingers. The tension hung thick in the air.

Then came the seventh inning stretch, a moment of respite and tradition as fans across the stadium stood to sing "Take Me Out to the Ball Game." After a rousing cheer, Bill's voice echoed through the stadium speakers announcing the results of the drawing.

"Congratulations to Clay from Pasadena, California! You'll be the Dodgers Batboy for Sunday's game!"

A surge of emotions engulfed Clay as he absorbed the news. His family erupted into cheers, celebrating his triumph. The thrill of victory, however, was not confined to the drawing alone.

In the bottom of the ninth inning, with the game tied, the Dodgers' star outfielder stepped up to the plate. With a lightning quick swing, he hit a walk-off single, scoring his speedy teammate from second base. The stadium erupted in joy, and Clay found himself caught up in a whirlwind of emotions. The Dodgers had clinched the game with a walk off hit, and Clay had won the coveted opportunity to be the Dodgers Batboy.

It was a night of double celebration, and as the fireworks lit up the sky above Dodger Stadium, Clay couldn't help but revel in the incredible turn of events.

4 THE DREAM

The night Clay won the drawing was a restless one. Anticipation coursed through his veins as Clay tossed and turned. When he finally drifted to sleep a vivid dream of baseball glory unfolded in his mind.

In the dream, the Dodgers found themselves in an extra-inning thriller, with every player exhausted and no substitutes left. Clay, the unsuspecting batboy, was called upon to pinch-hit—an unprecedented move. The crowd roared as the unknown batboy strode confidently to the plate, wielding a bat borrowed from the Dodgers' dugout.

The opposing pitcher eyed Clay with suspicion, delivering a pitch up and in that nearly grazed him. Unfazed, Clay adjusted his stance, and on the next pitch, he connected with the ball, sending it sailing for an opposite-field double. The crowd erupted, disbelief and awe mingling in their cheers.

Now standing on second base, Clay wasn't satisfied

with just a hit. A pass ball allowed him to steal third base with lightning speed. The stadium buzzed with excitement as Clay stood just 90 feet away from home plate. On the next pitch the batter sent the ball soaring into the outfield for a potential sacrifice fly. Clay awaited the catch with the precision of a seasoned base runner and then raced home to score the game-winning run.

As he reached home plate, the dugout emptied, and his teammates sprinted to congratulate him. But just as the dream reached its peak, reality intervened. Clay's mom gently shook him awake.

"Time to rise and shine, Clay. Your travel team has a game today," his mom announced with a warm smile.

As the dream faded from his mind, Clay tried to shift his focus to his upcoming game. Yet, the knowledge that he would soon be the Dodgers Batboy continued to linger in his thoughts.

5 THE GAME

Clay's arrival at the Pasadena Pumas' game was met with an enthusiastic reception from his teammates. Word had spread like wildfire about his victory in the Dodgers Batboy drawing, and questions and congratulations buzzed through the air. During warmups, Clay reveled in the attention, beaming with pride as he shared the details of the trivia quiz earlier in the week and the announcement the night prior.

As the game kicked off, the tension in the air was palpable. The Pasadena Pumas faced off against the Long Beach Llamas in a nail-biting contest. In the second inning, the Llamas drew first blood, scoring a run after three consecutive hits. Down 1-0 with runners at the corners and two outs, a sharp line drive was sent hurtling towards Clay at third base. In a moment of brilliance, Clay made a spectacular play, snagging the ball and ending the inning.

Down by one run, Clay approached the plate in the

third inning with a chance to tie the game. A runner stood on second, and hope hung in the air. Clay connected with a line drive to the outfield, but his luck took a turn for the worse as the center fielder made a fantastic catch, then swiftly threw out the runner attempting to return to the base. Despite the unfortunate turn of events, Clay shrugged it off, thinking perhaps he was due for a bit of bad luck after his recent stroke of good fortune.

In the sixth inning, Clay found redemption. With the bases empty, he mirrored his dream scenario by hitting an opposite-field double. A subsequent hit from his teammate allowed Clay to round the bases, tying the game at 1-1. The rally continued as another batter sliced a ball into the gap driving in another run and putting the Pumas ahead 2-1.

The pressure heightened as the game reached its climax. In the last inning, the Pumas, now in the field, aimed to secure the win. However, a series of events unfolded against them—an infield hit, followed by two walks loaded the bases with two outs. Clay, usually focused on the game, caught a glimpse of Bill in the crowd with his son who was watching with wide eyes. Thoughts of his impending Dodgers Batboy adventure suddenly washed over Clay.

Just as Clay daydreamed about the following day, a sharp ground ball rocketed toward him. Startled back into reality, Clay dove for the ball, but it slipped past his glove. Two runs scored, and the Pumas suffered a heartbreaking loss.

6 THE BATBOY DEBUT

Clay awoke the next morning with mixed emotions. The sting of the travel game loss the previous day lingered, but today held the promise of a new challenge. Although the Pasadena Pumas had lost on Saturday, the Dodgers had beat the Giants—so today his favorite team was looking to close out an impressive series sweep and Clay would be right there on the field for it.

Eagerly, Clay and his family made their way to Dodger Stadium. The bustling energy of the stadium enveloped him as he entered, a sea of Dodger blue swirling as fans were arriving. Clay was swiftly escorted to the Dodgers' clubhouse, where a custom Dodgers uniform awaited him, emblazoned with the iconic Dodgers script text.

With a mix of nerves and exhilaration, Clay prepared for his debut. The uniform fit perfectly, and the Dodgers cap sat proudly atop his head. As he stepped out into the corridor, he was met by the seasoned gaze of Dave

Roberts, the Dodgers' manager.

"Clay, welcome to the Dodgers family! We're thrilled to have you here. I hear you play third base for the Pasadena Pumas—impressive stuff. Today, you're not just a batboy; you're part of this team. Let's make it a day to remember!" Roberts's encouraging words resonated with Clay, injecting him with a sense of purpose.

On the field, the vibrant baseball diamond stretched out before him as Clay took in the sight of his baseball heroes during batting practice. He exchanged greetings with the players, a surreal experience for the young enthusiast. The air buzzed with camaraderie, and Clay felt like he was living in a dream.

Game time arrived, and Clay assumed his role with diligence, grabbing bats and batting gloves for the players. The Dodgers, still locked in battle with the Giants, faced a daunting 5-0 deficit early on. The determination to salvage the series sweep hung in the air, and Clay sensed the collective will of the team.

In a surprising move after the fifth inning, Roberts approached Clay with a strategic idea to change the team's fortunes. "Clay, we need a spark. How about we switch things up? I want you near third base as our ballboy by the left field foul line. Being a batboy is great, but with your skills you might be better suited as a ballboy. Chase down those foul balls, get them back in play to the pitcher when he's doing well, and toss them into the stands if the pitcher wants a new ball. Let's turn the tide."

Excitement surged through Clay as he embraced his new role. Positioned near third base, he focused on his task, chasing down foul balls with fervor. As he glanced toward the third baseline seats, a familiar face caught his eye among the sea of fans—Bill and his son, cheering on the Dodgers, just a few feet from Clay's newfound ballboy station.

6 THE FOUL BALL

As fate would have it, Clay's strategic move to the third base foul line proved to be a game-changer for the Dodgers. The young Dodgers' pitcher, who had faced early struggles, found his rhythm, unleashing hard fastballs and confounding sliders that left the Giants' bats floundering. The only contact they managed were weak foul balls, precisely in Clay's vicinity. Like a seasoned fielder, Clay became a vacuum for these wayward balls.

With each foul ball, Clay demonstrated his agility, firing balls back into play or tossing them into the stands with a practiced ease. His diligence even allowed him to share a moment of joy with Bill's son, tossing him a foul ball that made the young boy's face light up with pure delight.

The Dodgers offense soon woke up, orchestrating an electrifying 6-run rally in the eighth inning. Two home runs, including a grand slam by their star first baseman, catapulted the Dodgers into the lead. Clay, immersed in the crescendo of the stadium's cheers, found himself in the heart of the baseball magic he had always cherished.

As the game teetered on the edge, the Dodgers' closer entered the fray in the top of the ninth inning for a nail-biting attempt to secure the 6-5 lead. Two quick outs brought the tension to a boiling point, but the Giants' speedy shortstop hit a triple down the right-field line, suddenly representing the tying run just 90 feet away. The next batter, the Giants' powerful first baseman, painstakingly forced a full count of 3 balls and 2 strikes, intensifying the drama.

The next pitch held its own twist of fate. A vicious swing met an off-speed pitch, and a screaming foul ball was sent hurtling towards Clay at over 100 miles per hour. In a breathtaking display of athleticism, Clay dove horizontally to snag the ball out of mid-air, a moment of sheer brilliance that left the crowd momentarily silent. Clay had not only made an incredible catch but potentially prevented a fan injury. As the applause erupted, Clay looked back, realizing that had he missed, the ball would have rocketed into the stands where Bill and his son were seated.

Dusting himself off, Clay jogged back to his station, basking in unexpected applause. Bill, still processing the close call, called out, "Hey Clay, you may have just saved us, buddy! What a catch!" As Clay soaked in the praise, he refocused on the game. The count was still 3-2, and with a determined windup, the closer unleashed a high fastball. The Giants slugger took a colossal swing, but the ball landed with a thud in the catcher's mitt.

"Strike three!" declared the umpire, and with that, the Dodgers completed the sweep. The stadium erupted in cheers, and Clay, still reeling from his sensational catch, realized he had not only lived out his dream but had become an unexpected hero in the Dodgers' triumphant series.

7 THE FAMOUS BALLBOY

On the ride home, Clay and his family relished the Dodgers' victory while listening to the post-game radio show. After discussing the key plays in the game, the broadcasters couldn't contain their amazement at Clay's extraordinary catch on the foul ball in the top of the ninth.

"I'm telling you right now, folks, I've never seen a ballboy make a play like that. Truly incredible reflexes to snag that line drive," exclaimed one broadcaster.

"You're exactly right about that. My jaw dropped to the floor here in the radio booth—whoever that kid is sure made his mark on the ballpark tonight," echoed the other broadcaster.

Clay, riding the wave accomplishment, went to bed that night and slept like a baby. The cheers of the crowd, the praises on the radio, and the acknowledgment of his exceptional play echoed in his dreams.

The next day brought a delightful surprise. Clay received a call from one of his Pasadena Pumas teammates. "Hey Clay, you should turn on the Weekly Recap show on SportsNet. They're doing a countdown of the best plays of the week, and you're on it!"

Eagerly, Clay rushed to the TV, tuned to the sports channel, and there he was—a clip of his catch was playing over and over again. The sports anchor exclaimed, "Here it is, the number one play of the week happened just last night. The Los Angeles Dodgers ballboy makes a catch for the ages on a foul ball. Awesome glovework!"

Clay couldn't believe it. His play was famous! Later that day, another phone call came—this time from Bill. "Hey Clay, thanks again for snagging that ball last night. I'm certainly glad to be unscathed! Look, everyone here at the Dodgers was super thrilled at how you handled yourself. You were a great batboy and ballboy! How would you like to be the ballboy for the rest of the home games this season?"

Speechless at first, Clay found his voice and accepted on the spot, with just one condition. "Bill, I would love to be the Dodgers ballboy, but some days I may have a travel ball game. Is it okay if I play for the Pasadena Pumas when that happens?" Bill quickly assured Clay that his commitment to the Pumas and his teammates would always come first.

And so, Clay became the Famous Dodgers Ballboy. When he wasn't manning third base for the Pumas, he was the agile and energetic ballboy for his favorite team. He forged deep friendships with the players, and they came to rely on him for games of catch during each pregame. As the travel ball regular season concluded a few weeks later, the Pumas finished on a winning streak, and Clay, shining at third base, was unanimously selected as the Most Valuable Player by his coaches.

Thrilled by his team's success, Clay now looked forward to the Pumas' chance to compete in a major playoff tournament in Northern California. Fate smiled upon him as, during the tournament, the Dodgers had a series against the Giants, this time at Oracle Park. So, after his tournament games, Clay would don his Dodgers uniform on enemy turf in San Francisco. The famous ballboy was more than overjoyed; he was living out a dream that transcended the foul lines and brought him closer to the heart of the game he loved so dearly.

Made in the USA
Las Vegas, NV
16 March 2025